ZORA'S TRAVELS

Zora's Travels

IRYNA COLVIN-SPENCER

PERSONAL DEDICATION

*This book is dedicated to Roczen, a young lad of two
with a beautiful smile that captured my heart.
Also, to Roczen's family, his grandmother Danielle, and
great grandmother, Gail. It was truly a blessing that you
were brought into our lives. Who would have thought the
high-five connections shared between Roczen and Zora
would be the catalyst to newly forged friendships?*

*I would also like to include my gratitude to my entire loving
family, who encourage me to keep pursuing my dreams.*

*To all those who believe as I do, that the animals
we adopt are an integral part of our family, and
deserve loving care, protection and a safe home.*

Zora's Dedication

I'm dedicating this book to my entire family. How fortunate I am to have all of them in my life. They all hold a special place in my heart. They say I have unconditional love, but they serve as a constant reminder of what unconditional love is all about.

I would also like to give a high five shout out to my new friend Roczen.

High Five! Wuff you! Zora

Please Donate to Animal Shelters everywhere.

Epigraph

*If you want to judge a person's character observe
how they interact with your children and pets.*

ACKNOWLEDGMENTS

To these special businesses below who offered great accommodations and hospitality.

A heartfelt thank you to Sandy and Tori of the Country Inn and Suites Radisson in Beckley, West Virginia.

Dustie, Circle K in Dobson, North Carolina

Tom, Manager from King's Courtyard Inn in Charleston, South Carolina.

Claire and Amy from Eli's Table in Charleston, North Carolina

June from La Quinta by Wyndham, Melbourne Viera, Florida

April from La Quinta Inn and Suites, Perry, Georgia

Nuemis from La Quinta by Wyndham, Clarksville, Tennessee

Randy from La Quinta by Wyndham, Mansfield, Ohio

To family and friends who offered their hospitality and some memorable moments.

Anna and Steve, Helen and Jay of DeBary, Florida

Robert Michael (Mike), Larry and Bruce

Mary (Maria) and Paul, Marge (Lulu), Tom and Judy (Rudy), Roger and Brian (Echo),

Lori, Kathryn and Sally

Eva and Dance, Mary (Maria) and Joe, Sheila and Steve (Sevy), Frank.

Sheila, mother of Aiden and Skylar

Wendy, her daughter Bailey, grandchildren Krash and Peyton, and their friend William

Thank you all for the memories

A special thank you to Becky, of "The Grooming Post", Elma, New York, who has kept Zora groomed to the nines.

FREE AT LAST

You may know from my previous book, Zora's Letters, that I was adopted. It was devastating to be told by my previous owner that I wouldn't amount to much and that she only purchased me to be a show dog to make her some money. They kept me locked up in a crate. It was love at first sight when I met my soon to be family.

My new human parents traveled a little, and I vacationed at my "Sissy's" (Julianne, my mommy's human daughter), with her family, and fur babies. They are all good to me and treat me like family.

Mommy and Lee said they would take me traveling with them the next time they planned a getaway. Thanks to the COVID pandemic, my plans were curtailed. I was told the only way I could travel was to wear a

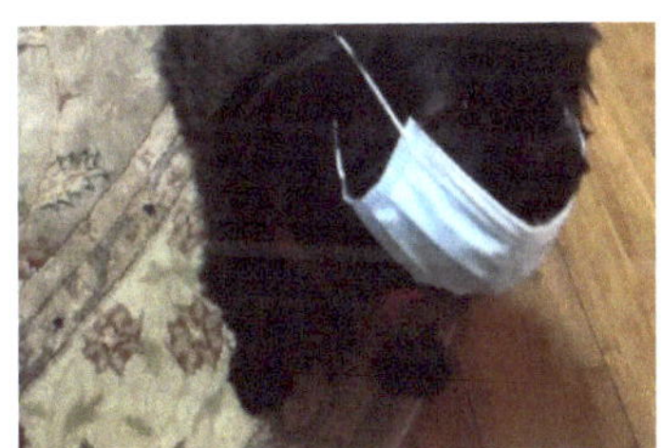

mask. Unfortunately, that wasn't about to happen because I couldn't breathe through the mask and had to wear the mask below the nose. I'm a Shih Tzu, and I don't have much of a nose to begin with. This was the best I could do to mask up, and that was unacceptable.

These past two years have been really hard. We were limited to where we could go. Winter came and went a couple of times. Living in the western New York area, winters can be quite brutal, and the wind chills penetrated my bones. All the hair on my body does nothing against those elements. I so wanted to go down to where it was sunny and warm.

My human parents promised me that when the restrictions were lifted, we would be on the road to see a lot of different places. I would check in and out of the pet friendly hotels. I didn't know they had hotels for pets, but then, how would I know that? I never really traveled outside of the western New York area. I got to stay a lot at my sissy's place when my parents traveled, and that was about the extent of my traveling experience, unless you call the veterinarian and groomer's a traveling experience.

I can't believe it's taken this long for me to live up to the promise I made in my last book, *Zora's Letters*. I promised to let my fur relatives know what it's like to travel in our great big country.

My first trial run trip with my parents was to Branson, Missouri. I had the whole backseat to myself and was grateful when my parents pulled over so that I could relieve myself. The first dog-friendly hotel we stayed in was a Hampton Inn in Dayton, Ohio. Everyone was nice and greeted me by petting me and saying how cute I was. It was late at night when we arrived; I was so tired, and I really wasn't in the mood for being charming. Despite that, everyone was so nice that I didn't want to disappoint them, and I even did my begging routine for them. That was the catalyst to my getting extra doggy treats. Works every time. I wanted to prove to my parents I would not be a bother, and they both assured me I wasn't.

We had reservations at the Gazebo Hotel, which welcome me with open arms. I found out, before too long, that there weren't many places where fur babies like me are welcomed, unless you are a service dog.

I must admit the hotel was very nice, and everyone there was very kind to me. It was my first experience in a hotel. I was told if I behaved myself, they would definitely take me on other trips. The fact that I behaved in the car, and didn't distract my daddy from driving, was a big plus. At least, that's what I was told.

My parents attended a convention, which they had both been excited about. Well, I know for sure Mommy was, and Daddy said we were just coming along to keep her company. Before too long, daddy was as much, if not more, involved than mommy was. He was the one buying souvenirs and telling mommy about the others he was interested in.

Unfortunately, Daddy somehow contracted food poisoning, which cut that trip short. He didn't want to see a doctor in Branson and only wanted to get back to see his own physician. Mommy packed up the car, and we were on our way. Mommy made sure she gave Daddy plenty of liquids to flush out his system, and midway home he was feeling better. We pulled into a Hampton Inn outside of Akron, Ohio, and mommy was grateful they allowed fur babies. There was a hefty fee because of me. Mommy was grateful that Daddy was feeling better and just wanted him to get some rest. The rest of the trip was uneventful; it was actually boring.

When we got home, I was told we would take a trip to Florida and promoting mommy's new book about her mom. She said we would visit relatives along the way. Yippee, a real vacation coming up for me.

THE ROAD TRIP HAS BEGUN

Hi Roxy,

It's really happening. We are packed and are ready to go. I know we are going to be gone a long time because I even have my own luggage and not just a bag that Mommy throws things into like she does when I come stay at your home. I have a place mat, new dishes to eat from, my own blankie, a few of my favorite toys, a BIG bag of dog food, plenty of my treats, and my protective bed blanket, which is reinforced with a waterproof shield on the back side in case I get too excited and have an accident. Now, that bed blanket ticked me off a little. I have not had an accident since the first week that I was adopted, and that was because I was nervous.

I am finally going to be traveling to Florida. Daddy is driving, and Mommy finished making all the hotel reservations. First stop will be the Radisson Country Inn and Suites in

Beckley, West Virginia. I'll tell you all about it when we get there.

So far, the ride has been boring. I'm in the backseat and can only see the sky through the front window and grass and trees out the side windows. We stopped in Meadville, Pennsylvania, for brunch. My stomach is a bit queasy. I think it's because I thought I was going to be left behind. I should have guessed they were taking me when I got a new halter and a new flea and tick collar. Like that's supposed to make me happy. It made the parents happy. I will write you more later. This is just the first few hours of the trip, but I thought I'd better jot it down before I forget.

Wuff you, High Five.

Good evening, Roxy,

Wow. Except for the long eight-hour drive, it has been fun. We made it to our hotel, Country Inn and Suites Radisson in one piece, despite the complaints my parents had about the crazy drivers on the road. We arrived at 5:45 p.m., not that time means anything to you. I just want you to feel like you are taking the trip with me. At the reception desk, a young woman named Tori greeted us. We found out on our arrival that Tori is Sandy's daughter, the woman my mommy spoke to earlier on the phone who took our reservation. A reservation is when you ask them to save you a room. Anyway, Tori came right over to me and gave me a hug. She said she was looking forward to meeting me. Tori told us she has a dog, Luna, two cats, and she also told me she loves animals. I  let her hug me because she was so nice. She also writes poetry and is studying to become a teacher. She told Mommy she didn't know when she would write a book. Mommy told her to never give up on her dreams.

I looked around to see if there were other fur babies. I could smell them, but couldn't see them. Maybe they got there earlier, or were getting there later. Tori gave us the key to our room. As soon as the door was opened, I saw that there was a couch just for me. Well, it was for all of us, but I made sure my parents knew it was mine first. Nice size rooms. After Mommy and Daddy put my place mat down and put some food and water out for me, they left me to go out for their dinner. They went to the Cracker Barrel restaurant next door that Tori told them about. This hotel has continental breakfast, but not dinner. I was a little nervous about staying alone, but I calmed down. Watching television helped. My parents weren't gone long, and they brought back some yummy turkey for me. Then Mommy took me for a walk. All this driving, the activity, and the meal relaxed me so much that I'm starting to close my eyes. I am sending a picture of Tori and me before I pass out. I am so exhausted from traveling. Doesn't Tori look sweet?

Good night, Wuff you, High Five.

Hi Zora!

I'm glad you're having fun and going to Florida. If you were a nice cousin, you would have invited me to come along. We have plenty of snow out here today. I like the snow and cold. As you already know, I'm an American Eskimo so l really enjoy rolling around in all the white, fluffy snow. It feels so good and cools me off. I could stay outside forever! I don't like long car rides. They upset my tummy, but who knows, I might have been able to get over it, especially if you were with me. I hope you feel better.

Wuff you too!

Good morning, Zora.

I thought I'd write to you first because my Mommy has a busy schedule planned. Not for me, but for herself. It's pierogi time, and you know what that means. Your life and mine, as we like it, are put on a back burner, except for food, and being put outside to do our thing.

I'm glad you're having fun. I am not having a good day, so far. I know you didn't like Jingles, my cat brother, but l really miss him. He went to heaven, and I haven't been able to see him since he left. Heaven must be far away. My family got me a new cat sister, and she's so mean. Her name is Pepper. She doesn't play with me like Jingles did. Whenever I fall asleep, she runs up and paws my face and runs away. That's not a fun way to be woken up. My mommy tells her to stop, but she doesn't listen. Pepper was getting ready to attack me again, so Mommy stayed with me on the couch to protect me. I'm going to try to take another nap. I'm so tired from being constantly woken up. Who says cats are fun?

Have fun!

Wuff you!

Good morning, Roxy,

Sorry it took so long to respond to your text, but it has been a very busy day. I had breakfast at the Radisson, and my parents met Sandy, Tori's mother. She also runs the check-in desk at the hotel and is very nice. She reminded me of Tori, and I let her hold me, too. There is no doubt in my mind that they welcome fur babies in this hotel with these two people greeting guests. Sandy told Mommy a lot about her daughters' dreams, and Mommy told her to keep encouraging Tori. After meeting Tori, she had no doubt Tori had both feet planted on the ground. Okay, I must admit, that statement puzzled me. Where else would her feet be? We said our goodbyes to Sandy and left. I'm sending you a picture of Sandy with me, so that if you ever travel, you will know what she looks like.

Wuff you. High five.

CHARLESTON, SOUTH CAROLINA BOUND

Hi Roxy,

It took us a little longer than I expected to get to our next destination, which is the King's Courtyard Inn in Charleston, South Carolina.

We had to pull off the road to get some gasoline because we were running low. Mommy made a comment that she really wanted to wait till we got to our hotel, because you never know how dirty the restrooms are along the way. Daddy pulled into the Circle K in Dobson, North Carolina. While he was filling the car with gas, Mommy went inside. All I have to say is she was there for quite some time. When she came out, she had a big smile. It seems mommy was pleasantly surprised. The whole little quick stop store was spotless, as were all the facilities. She told the young lady, Dustie, that her observation was that this was one of the cleanest and friendliest pit stops so far. Knowing mommy, she probably talked the young girl's ear off. Mommy loves cleanliness, almost to a fault. Mommy told her she was writing a book, and would definitely mention this as a great pitstop for travelers.

After feeling confident that we had plenty of gas and snacks, and I relieved myself, we were back on the road. Not only did the pit stop set us back a bit, but Daddy exited off the highway too soon because he was gawking at an accident on the other side of the road and missed our turn. To be fair, the co-pilot, Mommy, was also gawking, so she didn't let daddy know we missed the turnoff until it was too late. We ended up going across the two-and-one-half-mile Arthur Ravenel, Jr. bridge twice. There was nowhere to get off or turn around. The view from this extremely high bridge was beautiful, so the accidental, unexpected detour was well worth it.

When we finally got to the hotel, I ran toward the grass. Whew, that was a well-needed relief.

The city of Charleston is huge and busy. It was great to see all the hustle and bustle in downtown Charleston. They have rickshaw drivers (it's one person pulling a buggy with people inside), tricycle taxis, and horse-drawn carriages.

My impression of when we pulled up to the Kings Courtyard Inn in South Carolina was wow. They truly encased the hotel in one enormous courtyard. Cobblestone roads, various shops, and offices sat within this private courtyard. It's really beautiful here. The manager, Tom Moorman, stayed a little a longer at the hotel to greet me. He came right up to me and called me by name, telling me he looked forward to meeting me after hearing about me from my mommy. Then he looked at my parents and apologized because he didn't remember their names. Now that's when you know you're special.

Before we went in, Daddy took a picture of Mommy and me entering the hotel. There was another gentleman at the desk when we walked in. I didn't catch his name because I was too busy looking around. I heard mommy telling daddy he is the concierge. This friendly gentleman greeted us, signed us in, told us about the best restaurants in the area, how to get there, and then gave my parents the keys to our private carriage house room, which was on the second floor just outside the main entrance.

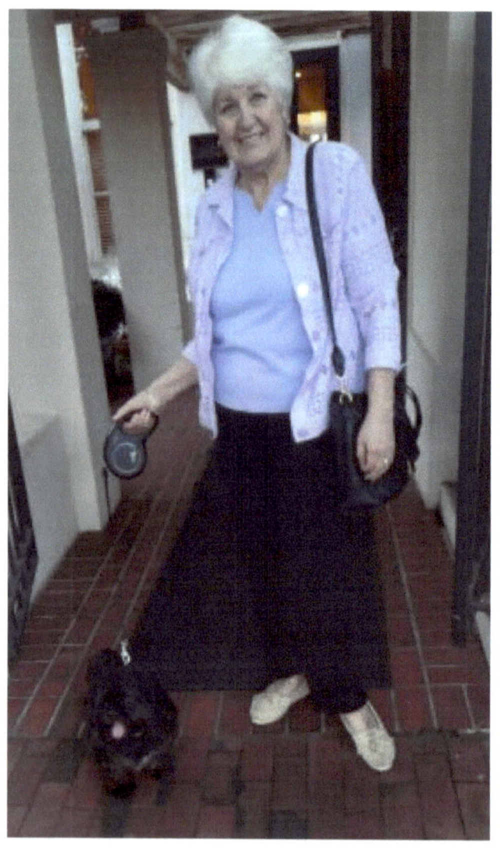

We have a huge, beautiful room. It has a king size bed and a chest of drawers to match, and the room also has a tele-vision, a refrigerator, a huge walk-in shower, and it's super clean. I was so looking forward to jumping on the bed to get some sleep because I was tired from the trip. I could tell that would not happen because my leash was still on.

Then we all left the hotel to walk over to get something to eat at Eli's Table on Market Street, which was recommended to us by the concierge. I enjoy saying that word, concierge; it makes me feel smart. It was just a short walk from the hotel. They allow dogs to eat there, outside, of course. Daddy had a scrumptious looking roasted chicken. Mommy and I shared a mouth-watering, perfectly prepared 8 oz. filet, which was just enough for both of us, though I think mommy ate the bigger portion. She didn't fool me for one minute that we were sharing it equally.

Claire, our server, gave me water in a China bowl. Amy, the manager of the restaurant, came out to meet me. They really know how to treat everyone. They were very nice, and the restaurant gets five stars from all of us. That means they are excellent.

Anyway, there were many people passing by, and I received plenty of attention. It was all about me, as it should be. Daddy took pictures of Amy and Claire holding me. My parents shared the dessert and told me I wasn't allowed to have any because it had chocolate in it. Now, I don't know who really made that decision, but Mommy told Daddy she read chocolate was not safe for dogs to eat. That didn't upset me too much as Claire gave me a special treat, a biscuit.

We walked back to the hotel, and daddy and I crashed. We were both dog-tired (pardon the pun). Mommy took pictures of us on the bed. I will share all the pictures that we took with you. That way, you will feel like you are with us.

I must say, everyone is really very friendly here. Having a very private room in the carriage house was just what we needed for a good night's sleep. We were thoroughly exhausted from walking almost all the streets of downtown Charleston.

Wuff you. High Five.

Hi Roxy,

I can't believe this is day three of our trip already.

The continental breakfast at Kings Courtyard was a sit-down meal, and my parents told me they ordered off the menu. Of course, because the dining was inside the restaurant, I wasn't allowed to go. Mommy told me that was the first time she experienced an elaborate, sit-down, continental breakfast where you order your breakfast off an extensive breakfast menu. She told me later that usually, the hotels let you help yourself to the continental breakfast, which is almost always buffet style. Even though I didn't go down, Mommy brought me some food, which she mixed with my food.

After we packed up, Daddy walked me into one of the court-yards. Mommy stopped in to speak with Tom, the manager, and let him know that we thoroughly enjoyed our room and the hotel. She said the hotel grounds were beautiful. Tom then went to give me a hug, and Mommy took a picture of him. No doubt he likes fur babies, and he smells nice, too.

He took Mommy and me into another courtyard that Mommy had not earlier seen. It had a lion head fountain, and Mommy told Tom that her brother, Mike, was a collector of lions. Tom took a picture of Mommy holding me near the Lion Head fountain, but Mommy told me later she's not sending that one out. She whispered to me that when we get back; we are both going on a diet. I guess that means she didn't like the picture.

Hello Zora!

Glad you're having so much fun. It finally warmed up to 68 degrees here in the Buffalo area today. It is so windy that the wind was knocking me down when l went outside. We had a full house here yesterday. Michala and Mommy both had a few friends over. Aunt Cheryl was here, and she always brings me treats. Mommy made homemade chicken soup, and it was delicious. I love when she makes the soup because she freezes some in ice cube trays and gives them to me on hot summer days. That's one thing I really like about summer. Pepper has been behaving, which is good. Mommy filled a squirt bottle with water and sprayed her when she bothered me. She did not like that. I did because now I can sleep without her pawing my face. I'm going to go now and take a nap. I like my naps.

Wuff you!

PALMETTO CARRIAGE RIDE
THEN, SAVANAH, GEORGIA

Hello Roxy,

Before we checked out of the King's Courtyard Inn, Mommy had made reservations for all of us with Palmetto Carriage Works to take a carriage tour through Charleston. It was so much fun. Tommy was the driver and gave us a history lesson about Charleston's founders and the elite. He had the horse drive us up and down the streets of Charleston to see the buildings, and he explained all the history behind them. It was very interesting, for my parents, that is.

We were given the whole backseat of the carriage so that I had room to move around. A little boy that was around two years old sat in front of us with two ladies. The little boy turned around and smiled at me. He held out his hand, and I touched him with my paw, giving him my high five sign. Mommy then asked the little boy if he liked doggies.

He just smiled. Then mommy asked the woman on the right if her son did any talking. Mommy told her that her daughter talked almost as soon as she was born. I knew she was kidding, of course, or was she? Mommy smiled and said that her son didn't talk until he was two, and she thought it was because his sister did the talking for him.

The lady introduced herself to Mommy as Danielle, and she said she was the young boy's grandmother, whom she introduced as Roczen. She explained young Roczen had a stroke when he was five days old. Not only that, he lost his mother over a year ago. Danielle explained that when Roczen gave me his hand in an upward position, that was his high five sign. That was the exercise he was taught in therapy to gain mobility in his right hand. Mommy smiled and said that was amazing. When I gave my paw in the same upright position, that was my high five sign. That's the sign off signal I used in my previous book, *Zora's Letters*. Mommy explained that was the first sign she could teach me when she adopted me at five months old, and the only command I easily responded to. Mommy explained that asking me to give my paw didn't work. She explained I was a rescue dog, and that I initially had a hard time adopting to my new home. They had crated me for most of the five months of my life. How uncanny, she said, that both Roczen and I used the high five signs as a greeting.

Mommy told Danielle that Roczen had the most beautiful smile when he turned around to look at me. She said he stole her heart. (Now, that is a phrase I had never heard before. How can your heart get stolen? Isn't it inside your body?)

Danielle told us more. She said that after losing her daughter, Roczen's mother, she took on the responsibility of caring full time for her grandson. She did his therapy exercises with him and attended to him around the clock. Danielle then introduced us to the other woman that was sitting on the other side of Roczen, as Gail, his great grandmother. Gail said Roczen was very fortunate to have a grandmother that was also a nurse. Mommy replied that was exactly the love and tender loving care he needed. He also was fortunate to have the undivided medical attention by a professional nurse.

Mommy then asked Danielle if she wouldn't mind if we got a picture of Roczen with her holding him, Tommy, our driver, our horse, and me. Mommy told her that when the book came out, she would send a copy to Roczen so that he would have it as a keepsake.

Daddy took the picture, and we walked away from the stable because other people were lining up for the ride. Mommy then asked if anyone remembered the horse's name? None of us did, so Mommy said she would try to find out from the booking agent. Unfortunately, no one could provide us with the horse's name, and as I thought it was just a bigger dog, I wasn't too interested.

We all walked out into the yard to get away from everyone. Mommy told Danielle she would send Roczen a copy of each of the books she had written when we got back home. Danielle gave mommy her address so that they could keep in touch.

We said our good byes, and Mommy promised to keep in touch with Danielle.

The drive to our next stop, Savannah, Georgia, was only a few hours long. We ended up on the outskirts of Savannah at the Holiday Inn. The drive wasn't that long, but we hit pockets of heavy traffic.

When we pulled up to the Holiday Inn, the desk clerk was far from cordial. After being told that they would not honor the confirmed reservation, Mommy was quite upset. Things got a little better when Mommy asked them to contact the hotel manager so that they could rectify the problem. After what seemed like forever, the manager on the other end finally agreed to honor the price for the Savannah Hotel, but not for the hotel we reserved in Melbourne. Well, that was the end of any future stay at that hotel.

Unfortunately, that episode and the rainy day prevented us from seeing much of Savannah. Mommy and Daddy had been there before, but I had not and was looking forward to it. Mommy told me maybe next time. The light bulb went off in my head. That means they are planning on taking me on more trips. Yippee.

Needless to say, there's not much more I can write. The hotel was adequate, nothing interesting to write about. Based on our experience, Mommy said the hotel didn't deserve any reviews. Hopefully tomorrow will be a better experience.

Wuff you. High Five.

DEBARY AND MELBOURNE, FLORIDA

Good morning, Roxy,

I just noticed I have heard nothing from you for a day or so. Here it is, March 4th, and not one word from you in a couple of days. Who's counting? I miss not hearing from you. Actually, I wouldn't have known what day it was if Mommy hadn't looked at her phone to tell Daddy, because he didn't know either. It's a good thing they have cell phones to keep them up to date.

We checked out early and couldn't wait to leave. It's funny how one unpleasant experience can ruin a perfectly good day. Once we were packed, and in the car, Mommy looked at both Daddy and me and said, "Okay, we will put this experience behind us, as we have so much to look forward to."

What a whirlwind trip so far. We arrived in Debary, Florida, to visit Mommy's "adopted" cousin, Anna, her husband

Steve, and their good friends, Helen and Jay. Mommy knew Helen and Jay from the Buffalo area. Wow, you should have seen Anna and Steve's home! We could all move in and there would still be room left over. I think we could have stayed there, and no one would have been the wiser. It's that big. Lots of places to hide. Then they put all this food out for us to eat. It was truly a feast fit for kings. You would think they were feeding an army. I didn't know what to eat first. The adults kept eating, drinking, and laughing a lot. Thankfully, Steve kept petting me, rubbing me behind the ears, and also sneaking food to me.

They talked about the war that was going on in Ukraine, and how similar it was to the atrocities that were faced by their own parents during WWII. These four lovely people, together with members from their parish, St. Ann's Catholic Parish, and surrounding neighbors were collecting food, clothing, toys, many donations, including money for the people of Ukraine. We observed some of their hard work, and Anna told us there were going to be several large trucks getting these donations to the dock so that they could be shipped overseas. The more they talked, the more I snacked. All in all, looks like I'm the one that will have to go on a stricter diet. They all fed me, except for Mommy. I loved Steve's petting me, and I laid next to him most of the time. Mommy tried to get me to show off my tricks. I wasn't ready, (mostly from having a full belly), and I also figured if I was stubborn, we'd stay a little longer. It worked. Then, when we were ready to leave, I gave Anna and Steve a high five. As we headed for the car after what seemed like forever, everyone kept swiping their hand across their mouth and flinging it our way, and Mommy was doing the same. She said that was our way of throwing kisses. Not like us dogs. We get close, one quick sniff and lick, and out we go.

I settled in for a long ride as we were going to see Uncle Mike's restaurant in Melbourne. They aptly named it Hamburger Mikes. Yummy. Cousin Larry was there to greet us, and we met his best friend, Shelly. We also met Rachel, who works at the restaurant, and Robert, who worked in the kitchen and was kind enough to bring me water. He could tell I was thirsty because my tongue was almost touching the ground. I can't believe how thirsty I've been. It must be the heat.

 A short while later, Uncle Mike arrived at the restaurant, apologizing for not being there when we arrived. He explained he had been out making deliveries. We stayed there for a couple of hours, that is Daddy and I stayed there. Mommy and cousin Larry went to check out a few hotels, since the previous hotel refused to honor our reservation. After about an hour, Larry and Mommy returned and said they could actually find a hotel that was pet friendly. Mommy said she was getting a bit concerned because every hotel up till then was completely booked, and we could get the room in this hotel because of a last-minute cancellation. Lucky break for us. Even though this hotel was a bit further out from the restaurant, and my relative's home, Mommy said it was worth it, as her first impression was that it was spotless, and there were no telltale animal odors.

That was good news because by this time, I was exhausted. I kept pawing Mommy to wrap up the conversation so that we could get to our hotel. I wasn't used to these long days. It worked, and we drove to our hotel, La Quinta, by Wyndham in Melbourne. It was a very nice and clean hotel, as mommy had stated earlier. They actually had a place just for dogs where I could walk and relieve myself. Wow, our own special doggie toilet. They even had baggies available so that our parents could clean up after us.

When we came back into the hotel, we were greeted by the manager, June, who was very nice. Mommy told her how clean and odorless the hotel was. She told June she was impressed because you couldn't tell there were other pets staying there. I couldn't wait to get into the room, and I fell asleep as soon as my head hit the pillow, actually as soon as my head hit my blanket, the one mommy put on the bed for me, which had a waterproof backside just in case I had an accident. As if I would. Doesn't she realize by now I don't have accidents? She always says you can't be too careful. Oh well, it is what it is. Will write more later.

Wulff you, High Five.

Hello Roxy,

Well, another day in Melbourne. Mommy went to breakfast at some fancy place with Larry and his friend Shelly, and Daddy and I got to go to Mike's restaurant. Then when Mommy got back, Uncle Mike took us touring around the city. We ended up going to a flea market. No, they don't sell fleas. Actually, it's a big place with a lot of shops inside. The sign said that all dogs had to be pushed in a buggy. That wasn't about to happen. We stopped at a place that rented dog carriages, and I refused to be tethered inside. Then I noticed that quite a few people had their dogs on a leash, and they too, were walking all around the flea market, both inside and outside. My collar kept slipping off, so mommy picked up a new collar and leash for me, and would you believe it's purple?

After what seemed like forever, because Uncle Mike enjoys walking around the flea markets, we drove to their home. Remember how I told you I was looking forward to meeting their fur babies, my cousins Wesley and Justin? Well, not so much anymore. They actually tried to attack me. In all fairness, I let out a high-pitched sound when Justin came near me, and I might have shaken him up. I can tell you his growl scared the heck out of me. Daddy grabbed me, as I clawed at him, and put me on his lap. Then Uncle Mike, or Larry, at this point I wasn't sure which, locked up the fur cousins. Bruce, who is a friend of theirs and also lives there, made a comment that it was unusual for Justin to react that way because he was normally protective of smaller dogs. Well, I must be the exception, because he wasn't impressed with my small body. So much for getting to know my Florida fur cousins. You just can't pick family sometimes. Thank goodness they were locked for the rest of the time I was there. I was afraid I might be dessert.

Uncle Mike fixed dinner for all of us. Yes, I was included. The other fur boys got their food in their room. That's what they get for picking on someone smaller than them. The bullies! I was debating whether to be a stinker and prolong our stay, but then decided against it. I was tired, as it was a long day. We said our goodbyes, and made a farewell breakfast date for the following morning at Cracker Barrel, my mommy's favorite breakfast place. Actually, it's her favorite browsing place, as they have a lot of unusual items throughout their gift area. Who does she think she's kidding?

Breakfast would have been great for the adults, had our server brought the utensils before she brought the meals. The adults had to ask for the utensils. I had no problem. However, their meal was cooled down. Cold eggs, yucky. Other than that little episode, we spent our time saying out good byes, with promises to stay in touch along the way home.

Yippee, we got back into the car and headed for North Port to Aunt Mary and Uncle Paul's condo in Cocoa Plum. Mommy and I used to live there for a short time, and I am looking forward to reconnecting with my friends. Remember Roxy, I told you about them. Of course, you are still my best friend, and favorite female fur cousin.

Wuff you, High Five.

Go Zora!!!

Hope you're still having fun. Sorry to hear about the experience you had in the hotel in Savannah. We definitely will cross that off our list. Not that we are going anytime soon. Who am I kidding? I won't be doing any traveling! My traveling involves going to the vet, the groomer, and once in a while to Tim Hortons, where at least they treat me special with a Tim bit treat.

Sorry to hear about your experience with your Florida fur cousins. At least you and I have each other. Funny how it works sometimes. For us, it was an instant connection. Like we had known each other for years. I hear that's the way it works sometimes for humans.

We got snow the past few days, and it was so much fun rolling around in it. We are expecting a heat wave in a couple of days where the temperature will be about 60 degrees, and all the snow will melt. My mom thinks that was the last of the snow.

I got to go to Tim Hortons this morning and get a Timbit. When I'm a good girl during the week, that's my Sunday treat. They're so yummy and all the workers are so happy to see me. They know my name, and two employees always come by say hi. Sometimes, they give me extra treats.

There was lots of commotion here today. We lost power for a couple hours, and Mommy had a turkey in the oven. She was freaking out because if a turkey isn't fully cooked in 30 minutes, bacteria can grow on food and it's not safe to eat. Daddy put the turkey on the grill in the backyard for an hour. Fortunately, the power came back on an hour later, and Mommy could put it back in the oven. It turned out to be delicious.

Hope to see you soon so we can play.

Wuff you.

NORTH PORT, FLORIDA

Hi Roxy,

It was sure great hearing from you. This entire week has been a whirlwind. We went to North Port to stay with Aunt Mary and Uncle Paul. There were so many cars whizzing by on the I-75, I closed my eyes. I prayed we would get there safe, and in one piece. We saw one car, whose whole front end caught on fire when it hit the center divider. Mommy had spotted that same car speeding and weaving in and out of traffic earlier. We don't know if they saved the people in the car. Mommy blessed herself and said a prayer for them.

It was beautiful seeing the palm trees swaying in the breeze, and I had an entire week to destress. I reconnected with my good friend Lulu. She whispered that she really missed me. We sat huddled for a bit, like old times, and exchanged secrets, as only us fur gals can do. Lulu let me know she traveled a lot with Marge, her human mom. They shared a lot of special times, just like Mommy and I do. Lulu's human daddy passed away too, so she understood what I had gone through. She told me she likes Mike, Marge's good friend. He treats her well. She still is good friends with Rudy. He is a King Charles Spaniel and is quite handsome. I told her I couldn't wait to see him again. I really liked him a lot, and I hope he didn't forget me. We discussed we were getting older, and our bodies aren't as agile as they used to be.

Lulu is a seasoned traveler, and she gave me some tips about traveling. Making sure I had water, food, snacks, toys, a blankie to keep me warm. I told Lulu that Mommy did that for me. We admitted we were spoiled brats because we both got to eat at various restaurants.

A couple of hours later, while Daddy was walking me around the Coco Plum grounds, I ran into Rudy, my old heart throb. Mr. Tom, Rudy's daddy, was walking Rudy. We didn't need good eyesight to spot each other. I could spot Rudy's tail wagging a block away. His daddy and mine stopped to chat, while Rudy and I got reacquainted. Fortunately, his memory and his sniffer were as good as mine. We reconnected.

The following day, everyone was getting together at Marge's condo. Lulu didn't feel like coming out, so I spent a little time with her. Then I went outside where Tom and Judy were with Rudy, on a leash, of course. Condo rules. You would think humans would know by now, we dogs do not like rules. That aside, Rudy and I came right up to each other. Despite our limited restrictions, we still managed to lick each other. We huddled and amused our family. They all said how cute we were together. They were right, of course.

Rudy told me he didn't travel as much anymore, but he too had stayed at La Quinta Hotels when they traveled. We chatted awhile longer, while the adults all visited.

Mommy took pictures of me with Lulu, and then with Rudy. I told mommy I only wanted pictures with myself and Rudy, so it would appear that we were alone. With those crazy rules, we had to have pictures of the adults in there, too. My apologies to Tom and Judy, as Mommy had a hard time removing their feet from the pictures, and you can still see the leash.

I was free to roam at Lulu's home, so we could get close enough to whisper. The last time we met, we talked about how different it was where I lived, compared to Florida, where she spent most of her time. Lulu was the real traveler in our group, and I asked her if there was any place that she liked better than the other. She looked me right in the eye and said, "Home is still the best place to be. I know where everything is. I have the friendships that I have forged over the years. Unlike our humans, we fur babies know home is where the heart is, and my heart is here." I agreed with her on that point. Though I hadn't been traveling for too long, it was tiring. Don't get me wrong, I enjoy meeting all the new people and their fur babies, but it gets tiresome. Just like in the human world, we have certain members of our species who carry on like babies and are drama queens. If you don't pay them enough attention, they carry on. According to Mommy, I fit into that category. I must say, I disagree with her. I may be a bit spoiled, but I'm far from a drama queen. I'm just cute.

Roger was walking his beautiful dog named Echo, who was a new friend to me. At first, I didn't want to get close to him. He was a handsome dog, but I was upset with him because he lived in the condo that we used to own. He told me he loved living near the canal. Like me, he said he didn't like all the rules, but he tries to follow them. I asked him if he had come across the alligator that lived in the canal. He said he saw him, but fortunately their paths hadn't crossed. We talked about how the condo rules are different for us. The humans get away with everything. I warmed up to him a little, but I saw little of him. His owners, Roger and Randy, were nice enough to invite us in to see what they had done to our former condo. It was still beautiful, but mommy said the added touches made it that much more so.

Mommy took a picture of myself and Echo while we were walking around the condo grounds. The grounds are beautiful, but Echo was of the same mind as I was with Rudy. We hated being restricted on our leash. It's not like we are wild or anything. Heck, I was watching some adults, and they were rowdier than any of us fur babies had been.

Florida is beautiful, and warm. Mommy got to spend only one day in the pool, because the weather didn't quite cooperate. Despite that, there was so much to do. We went to Fisherman's Village, ate at the White Elephant, Gator, and Mama's Pizza. Okay, so I'm exaggerating a little. The adults got to go to the most of the restaurants, and eat there. They brought me the leftovers. I'm not complaining, mind you. The leftovers were quite tasty. Only a few of the places were fur baby friendly.

While the adults went out, I got to spend some time with my friend Lulu. We had our goodbye for now at breakfast with Aunt Mary and Uncle Paul.

Cannot believe that we already spent a week here. I was sad to say goodbye to my friends, not knowing when I would see them again. It's time for us to move on to our next stop, knowing that will bring us closer to home.

I will write more tomorrow.

Wuff you, High Five.

Happy St Patrick's Day, Zora!!!

I had a fun day today. I spent most of the day outside. It was 67 degrees here. Mommy put a green bandana on me, and all the neighbors walking by said how cute l looked. I did. The green against my white fur made me stand out. Of course, I looked much cuter to them after some of Mommy's and Daddy's friends had a few cocktails.

Can you imagine how much partying they will do when the official Saint Patrick's Day celebrations begin?

Our porch is all set up with the wicker furniture and outdoor carpet, and everyone is so happy to be outside. I can't wait to see you when you get home. Safe travels! Wuff you!

BELLAIRE BLUFFS

Hi Roxy,

It was great hearing from you. For a while there, I thought you forgot about me. We've had a hectic week, as you can well imagine from my previous text.

Monday, the day we left North Port, we went to a wonderful restaurant, Pier 22 in Bradenton. I was allowed on the patio, which was near the water, with lots of yachts and boats docked nearby. We met Mommy's friend Lori, though I had met her before at our home in Depew. She came with her daughters Kathryn and Sally Ann, whom I had never met. They were extremely nice to me. Then again, who wouldn't be? I can be quite entertaining when I want to be. I did my usual routine of being cute with my tricks.

The restaurant was beautiful; the girls were funny; I got plenty of attention, and great food was snuck my way. I was really full when we finally said our goodbyes because we had to leave to get to Belleair Bluffs before dark. It was great seeing Lori again and meeting her daughters. Too bad Daddy forgot his cell phone in the car, and we didn't get any pictures. Looks like this will just be a memory.

It took us a little over an hour to drive to Belleaire Bluffs to visit Mommy's adopted cousin, Eva and her husband Dance. Mommy said it was always party time when she visits there. Eva's sister, Mary, her husband Joe, and a friend Frank, who lives with Eva and Dance, joined us. Mommy hand-delivered an early birthday present from a mutual friend of theirs from back home. It was from Cookie, also known as Audrey. Cookie was Eva's best friend from Buffalo, as well as a friend of my mommy's. Eva and Mommy talked about how they all the ice skated in the fields which were across from their homes. Eva and Dance's daughter-in-law, Sheila, and their son Steve, stopped by to say hello. They brought with them their fur baby, Sevy, who wouldn't leave me alone for one minute. I swear he was obsessed with me. Every time I made any movement, he was right there beside me. Tiring, I tell you. I was so exhausted from trying to avoid him, I literally collapsed right after he left.

All the adults sat around talking about their youth and about all the good times they had growing up. Their parents and Mommy's parents were all close friends, more like family, Mommy used to say when talking about them. They reminisced well into the night, and then sadly, everyone had to leave. Well, if truth be told, I wasn't too sad about Sevy leaving.

The following day, Eva and Dance tried to talk Mommy and Daddy into staying longer, but they said they were on a tight schedule, and had to leave. We left amid lots of hugs and kisses goodbye, with promises that if we had the opportunity to come back within the next year or two, we would stay longer. Fortunately for me, no Sevy. He was at home with his family.

Once again, it was too late when we realized we were so engrossed in our conversations and spending time with each other that no one took any photos. Looks like our memory bank will have to capture the moments as best as they can.

Our next destination was only a couple of hours away. We went to Lake City to meet Daddy's great grandchildren. We met at a restaurant Mommy picked out called Gator's Dockside, which as it turned out was Aidan's, the great grandson's, favorite place to eat. Aiden was the older of the two great grandchildren, and fortunately for us, very talkative. Not a shy bone in his body. Skylar was younger and very shy.

As for me, I could not join them. It was raining so hard that I wasn't able to sit on the restaurants deck. That was another reason we chose that restaurant. Darn rain ruined a good meal for me. I was stuck with leftovers and dog food. Yuk.

Daddy said he really enjoyed spending time with his two great grandchildren, Aiden and Skylar, and their mother, Sheila. Mommy couldn't get over how much both kids had grown since the first time she met them over two years ago. Daddy was very sad about leaving them because he knew it would be a long time before he could see them again. I got to meet them for one moment, despite the downpour.

Our next destination was to the La Quinta Hotel and Suites in Perry, Georgia. Mommy remarked how pristine the place was. The floors shined, and a smiling young lady greeted us. This young lady showed she had class, because she greeted me first. She had a bubbly personality and was the perfect greeter. Despite our arriving late in the evening, and being dog tired, this young lady made you forget that for a brief period. Mommy talked to her for a bit to see if there was any where she and Daddy could go to get something to drink and maybe a snack. She advised us there was a Cracker Barrel nearby, so that's where Mommy and Daddy went.

I was so tired that I couldn't wait to go to sleep. The bed was big, soft, and inviting.

Wuff you. High Five.

Hi Zora,

It's been a long time since I wrote, and I'm sorry. You have no idea how I wish I were there, and you were here. It's pierogi making time, and I get put on the back burner. You have no idea how many times I have to bark to get myself heard, that I have to go outside. Yet, one little meow from that new four-legged spoiled cat, and you would think the queen herself showed up to grace us with her presence.

I'll take you any day of the week. We at least get along, and you're not a nuisance. I really don't know what anyone sees in this thing they call Pepper. Doesn't pepper make you want to sneeze? This one does.

The weather is getting warmer, and my mommy is in a frenzy trying to get the house spruced up. You know she can't do all the things she used to, so things get done, but it takes longer. That accident really did a number on my mommy. She hardly complains, but when she lets out a curse word, you know she's in a lot of pain. Those are the times I try to cuddle up to her to make her feel better. Humans need loving, too.

I love reading about your trip so far, and I can almost imagine being there. What is it humans say, "I'm living vicariously through you"? Keep sending me your letters.

Wuff you back.

PERRY, GEORGIA

Hi Roxy,

I was surprised to hear from you, finally. I understand. It's tough to write to me when your secretary doesn't have the time to take your dictation and is too busy making pierogi. In all fairness, Sissy does have her good days and bad days with her back.

At least for now, I have Mommy all to myself and she writes everything I tell her. Sometimes she tries to add her own spin to my words, but I put a stop to that. You know me well enough to know what I would say, or wouldn't.

After one of the best night's sleep, Mommy took me for a walk around the hotel. They actually had a very extensive walking area for fur babies. They had a stand that housed pickup bags with a garbage can underneath. Now this doggy toilet is the best maintained one I have come across. You could tell the manager runs a tight ship. The area is spotless. However, I can tell you by all the smells that filled my nose, there were plenty of dogs staying there, just no remnants that they were there. I only saw a couple of dogs during our stay.

Mommy met the manager of the hotel, who introduced herself as April. Mommy told her how impressed she was with the cleanliness of the place. Actually, Mommy said it was immaculate. All the staff were super friendly. This La Quinta had an extensive continental breakfast which was constantly being replenished.

Mommy and April spoke for quite some time, and Mommy asked April if she would mind posing for a picture with me. The lobby of the hotel had some beautiful modern art, and mommy thought it would be a great background for my picture. Once again, I was right, it's all about me.

April explained to mommy that all the hotels were individually owned, and the owners set the prices. She also told Mommy that they held nearby horse shows and dog shows at the huge stables and arena complex. She also advised mommy the next time we travel we should plan on staying a couple of days. There is so much to see that it would be worth it.

Mommy told April that all the La Quinta hotels so far were extremely pet friendly, and from their personal experience, she would highly recommend this hotel to people traveling with their fur babies. The trend since COVID is that more and more people are traveling with their pets, because during the lockdown, they all bonded more than ever before.

We said our goodbyes to April and thanked her for her hospitality. Mommy even invited April to Buffalo, where she would be more than welcome to stay at our place.

Next on our list was a stop in Clarkesville, Tennessee to visit Daddy's daughter, Wendy, her daughter Bailey, William, who was a friend of Bailey's. We also met Daddy's two great grandchildren, Krash, whom I had already met a couple of years ago at our home, and Peyton, whom I hadn't met yet.

Will fill you in on that trip tomorrow.

Wuff you. High Five.

Hi Zora,

You really are seeing quite a few states and a lot of La Quinta Hotels. Considering you have stayed in a couple of different ones too, let me know which ones you found the cleanest and best suited for our needs. Not that I plan on traveling any time soon. We are down to two cars, and my human mommy says she feels like an unpaid Uber service, or taxi.

Pepper, the cat, is behaving a bit better, but that's because she doesn't like the water squirted in her face when she misbehaves, especially when she attacks me. Other than that, nothing really new and exciting here. I promise to be better at writing back to you, but you know how that goes. I still need Mommy to write for me. I'm put on the back burner because either the cat gets in the way or they have people coming over.

Wishing I was with you right now.

Wuff you.

CLARKSVILLE, TENESSEE

Hi Roxy,

We finally made it to Clarksville. It wasn't that long of a ride, and at least the scenery along the way wasn't boring. Daddy spoke to his daughter, who requested we meet her family at Cheddars, one of their favorite restaurants in Clarksville. I was not allowed to go in, and mommy promised me she would give me an extra special treat when they got back to the car. I was okay with that since the weather was nice. They left the window open for me and, of course, left some water and snacks for me. Not only that, I had my favorite toy next to me. Mommy was right, they did not stay in the restaurant too long; it was less than an hour.

As everyone exited the restaurant, only Peyton and Krash came over to meet me. I had met Krash before, but Peyton was new to me. She was hugging Daddy, and he had the biggest smile on his face. That was the first time he had met Peyton in person, and she was a very precocious four-year-old. We all stayed outside for a little while, and then Daddy and his daughter made a breakfast date for the following day.

Mommy later told me about meeting Daddy's granddaughter, Bailey, and her life partner William, who was Peyton's father, at the restaurant. Daddy's daughter was also at the restaurant, but I had met her at our home when she came to visit Daddy. However, Mommy stressed that when Peyton saw Daddy, she went running over to him, calling out grandpa, and wrapped her arms around his legs. That's because he's so tall, and she's so small, she added. Daddy actually had a tear in his eyes. He was so glad to finally meet his little great granddaughter.

After we left the restaurant, we checked into our hotel, the La Quinta. The manager, Nuemis, who was extremely nice, greeted us to me. She and Mommy talked for a while. She told Mommy how much she loved dogs, and that her own little Shih Tzu had passed away a while ago, and she was still grieving over that. She said that we are the cutest dogs. Now with that statement, I have to agree, not saying you're not cute, but let's face it, we are different breeds.

Nuemis directed us to the doggy relief areas. There were multiple ones, and as in the other La Quinta Hotels, there were scoop bags and a disposal provided for the guests.

Despite that, I noticed that some people still didn't observe the request to pick up, whether it was trash or after us fur babies. Speaking on behalf of myself, and I'm sure other fur babies, we like to walk around where it's clean. The good thing about mommy is that she wipes my feet when I come in from the outdoors. She says you never know what I can pick up on my feet, and as I have a tendency to lick my paws once in a while, it's a good thing they are clean. Mommy makes people take off their shoes when they come inside, for the same reason. She always says, "You never know what people unintentionally track inside."

We had another good night's rest. Mommy got up early the next day and went to the continental breakfast bar and picked up some food for both of us. Daddy was meeting his daughter for breakfast and some alone time, which gave Mommy and me a chance to pack up. Of course, I really didn't pack, I just watched.

When Daddy got back into the room, we packed up and left. Mommy stopped by the desk to say goodbye to Nuemis and told her how pleased she was with our accommodations. Other than that, this trip wasn't that eventful for me. Daddy got to see his family, Mommy got to meet them, and as for me, other than that brief time with Peyton and Nuemis who fawned over me, it was a quiet stay.

We drove around Clarksville for a bit and then headed toward home. Mom said our final destination along the route home would be Mansfield, Ohio, where she had already booked a room at the La Quinta Hotel there.

Well, that's enough about me for now. Can't wait to hear from you. We will be home before too long, and I will catch you up on everything that I may have missed.

Wuff you, High Five.

MANSFIELD, OHIO

Hi Roxy,

This is it, our last day of the trip before we come home. Mansfield is a nice little town. We didn't really have time to explore is as we were all extremely tired when we checked

in. They greeted us at the desk by a nice young lady, Tonya, who as all the personnel before her, greeted me first, as it should be. After all, if not for me, we probably would have never stayed at La Quinta. Their reputation for catering to fur babies made them stand out. My human parents were extremely pleased with the facilities they provided for the fur babies.

This last stop is the best stop because we are only a few hours from home. There truly is no place like home. I will share a few of the photos with you, and this also gives me some time to reminisce. My only complaint is that we didn't take more photos of me with the family members and friends. If this trip were truly about me, wouldn't my mommy or daddy have done that?

Today we checked out of the hotel, and are headed home. Before long, I will visit with you, and share in-person my entire traveling experience. I am attaching the last photo of the trip, and want you to know, this truly was a great trip for me. I knew I could do it and do it as I did. I prevailed. This photo depicts how tired I truly am as I settle into my favorite couch and position.

See you soon, my favorite cousin.

Wuff you, High Five.